MY BASEBALL BOOK

For the _____ season.

YEAR

 HarperFestival
A Division of HarperCollins*Publishers*

My Name is _Jordan Peter Lavelle_

PLACE A PHOTO OF YOURSELF HERE

Positions I play: _All_ **Uniform Number:** _10_

Height: _____ **I bat** *(left or right)*: _left_ **I throw** *(left or right)*: _left_

Place of birth: _4"6_ **Age:** _9_ **Home:** _____

My rookie year was 19 _20 00_ **, playing for the:** _____

Some of my fans who come to my games are: _____

_____

The bat I use is a *(model, length, and weight)*: _____ **My glove is a:** _____

2

My Team is

PLACE A PHOTO OF YOUR TEAM HERE

My teammates are *(starting front row, left to right)*: _____

_____

_____

_____

Our coach is: Jimmy Cerone & Nick Cataflamo   **Our team sponsor is:** Conway, Lavelle & Finn

My Team's Schedule

OUR GAME SCHEDULE FOR THIS SEASON   **HOME/AWAY**

#		HOME/AWAY
1.		
2.		
3.		
4.		
5.		
6.		
7.		
8.		
9.		
10.		
11.		
12.		

DID YOU KNOW...

The first recorded baseball game was played on June 19, 1864 at Elysian Fields in Hoboken, New Jersey. Though people often credit Abner Doubleday with inventing baseball, most baseball historians now agree that its real father was Alexander Cartwright, whose 20 rules of play helped shape the game we know today.

Our toughest games will probably be against:_____

Their best players are:_____

My personal goals for this year are:_____

_____

Our Home Field is *Farm Field*

Use this picture to show the layout of your home field. Include any fences around the field, as well as the location of its backstop, dugouts or benches, bleachers, drinking fountain, and any other special features. Do you know the distances from home plate to the fences in left, center, and right fields? If you don't, pace them off at your next practice.

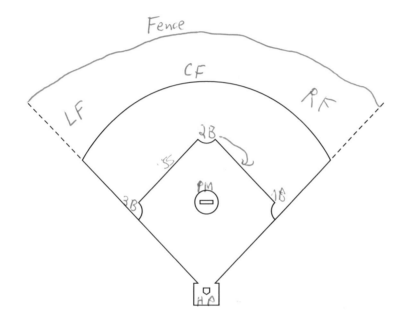

My home field's ground rules are *(if you don't know them, ask your coach or regular umpire)*: _____

_____

_____

What I like best about our home field is: _____

My Pregame Routine

If I eat a pregame meal, my favorite foods are: _____

_____

_____

_____

_____

_____

DID YOU KNOW...

Most big-league clubhouses provide post-game meals for their players. Typical dishes include lasagne, chicken, hamburgers, and barbecued ribs. If a player is thirsty he can go to the clubhouse cooler for a juice or soda, and if he wants bubblegum he can take all the pieces he'd like from the club-house gum jar.

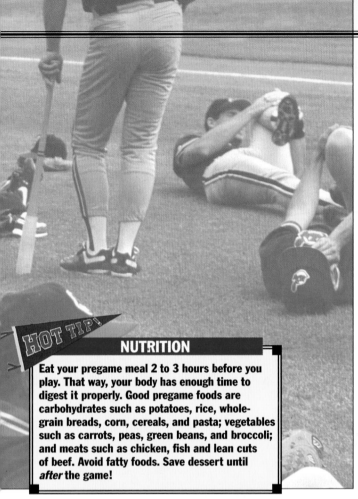

I usually get dressed in my uniform _____

_____ (minutes/hours) before game time.

When I arrive at the ballpark, the most important

things I always do are: _____

_____

_____

NUTRITION

Eat your pregame meal 2 to 3 hours before you play. That way, your body has enough time to digest it properly. Good pregame foods are carbohydrates such as potatoes, rice, whole-grain breads, corn, cereals, and pasta; vegetables such as carrots, peas, green beans, and broccoli; and meats such as chicken, fish and lean cuts of beef. Avoid fatty foods. Save dessert until *after* the game!

THREE PREGAME STRETCHES YOU CAN DO

1. To stretch your legs, stand upright, grasp one leg at the ankle and pull it slowly toward your butt. Hold for five seconds. This exercise will stretch the quadricep muscles in your thighs so you can bend easier when fielding grounders.

3. To stretch your torso, extend your arms as shown and gently twist your body at the waist. This will loosen your back and abdominal muscles for swinging the bat.

2. To loosen the calf and hamstring muscles in the backs of your legs for running, sit with one leg extended and one leg tucked underneath you. Lean forward and try to touch your toes. **GO SLOW!** Hold the stretch for five seconds, then do the other leg.

Our Usual Starting Lineup

Write in the names of your teammates

7 LEFT FIELD _Anyone_

8 CENTER FIELD _Anyone_

6 SHORTSTOP _Anyone_

4 SECOND BASE _Anyone_

5 THIRD BASE _Anyone_

1 PITCHER _Anyone_

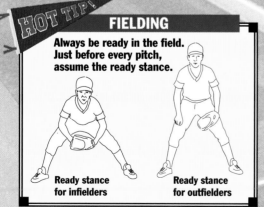

HOT TIP!

FIELDING

Always be ready in the field. Just before every pitch, assume the ready stance.

Ready stance for infielders

Ready stance for outfielders

2 CATCHER _Anyone_

8

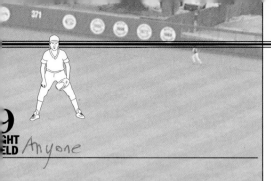

GHT
ELD Anyone

3
RST
ASE Anyone

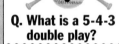

Each position on the field has a specific number (pitcher=1, catcher=2, and so on). Coaches, umpires, and sometimes radio and TV announcers will use these numbers to keep track of the game and record each play. A player's uniform number has nothing to do with the position he plays.

OTHER PLAYERS ON MY TEAM

10. _____

11. _____

12. _____

13. _____

14. _____

OTHER PITCHERS FOR MY TEAM

15. _____

16. _____

17. _____

18. _____

Q. What is a 5-4-3 double play?

A. With a runner on first, the third baseman (5) fields the ball, throws it to the second baseman (4), who steps on second and then throws to the first baseman (3), who steps on first.

DID YOU KNOW...

The average tarpaulin used in major league stadiums to cover the infield during rainouts weighs over one ton. When an infield gets wet, many major-league ground crews spread kitty litter on the basepaths to absorb moisture.

TEAMS   SCORE

_____ (HOME) VS. ☐

_____ ☐

The most exciting part of the game came in the

_____ inning. Here's what happened:

_____

_____

_____

_____

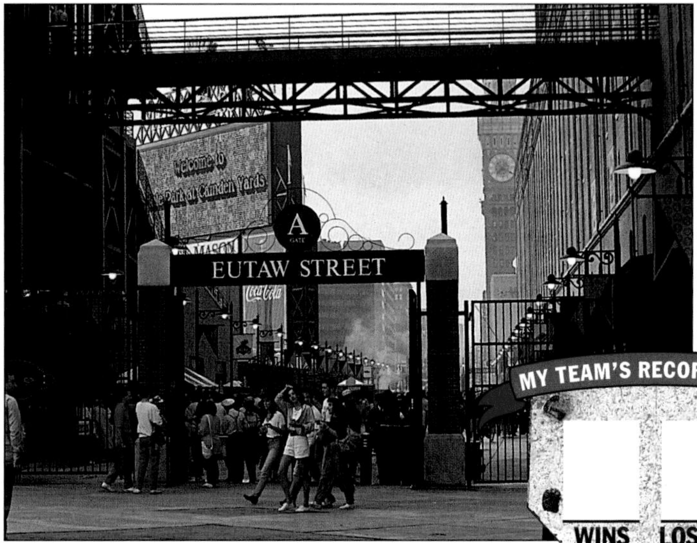

STARTING PITCHERS   THROWS R/L

_____ VS. _____

_____

WINNING AND LOSING PITCHERS

_____ Won

_____ Lost

IF YOU PITCHED, HOW WELL DID YOU DO?

I pitched _____ innings.

I struck out _____ batters,

walked _____ batters,

gave up _____ hits,

and _____ earned runs.

My earned run average (**ERA**) after one game is:

☐

(See page 35 for how to compute your **ERA**)

MY TEAM'S RECORD IS NOW

☐   ☐

WINS   **LOSSES**

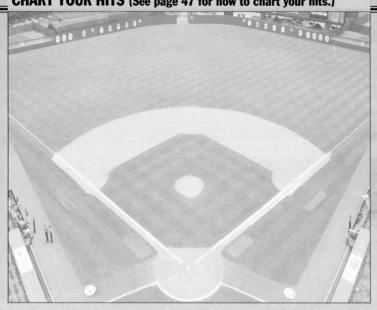

MY AT BATS

I batted _____ times.

I got _____ hits,

I walked _____ times, and

batted in _____ teammates.

I struck out _____ times,

grounded out _____ times, and

popped out _____ times.

My batting average (**AVG**) after one game is:

*(See page 39 for how to compute your **AVG**)*

IN THE FIELD

I played *(name position[s])* _____ .

I had _____ fielding chances.

I made _____ fielding errors.

I made _____ throwing errors.

My fielding average (**FA**) after one game is:

*(See page 37 for how to compute your **FA**)*

For our next game I

need to improve on:

_____

_____

_____

_____

HOT TIP! **THROWING**

When throwing a ball, grip it across the long seams and keep your throwing elbow up. Release the ball with a snap of your wrist and the rest of your arm following through.

TEAMS   SCORE

_____ (HOME) VS. [ ]

_____   [ ]

HOT TIP!

BATTING

Assume a comfortable stance with your knees bent, bat back. Keep the bat off your shoulder and don't waggle it! This way, you won't swing late at fastballs.

CHART YOUR HITS (See page 47 for how to chart your hits.)

The most exciting part of the game came in the

_____ inning. Here's what happened:

_____

_____

_____

_____

MY AT BATS

I batted _____ times.

I got _____ hits,

I walked _____ times, and

batted in _____ teammates.

I struck out _____ times,

grounded out _____ times, and

popped out _____ times.

My batting average **(AVG)** after two games is:

[   ]

*(See page 39 for how to compute your **AVG**)*

IN THE FIELD

I played *(name position[s])* _____ .

I had _____ fielding chances.

I made _____ fielding errors.

I made _____ throwing errors.

My fielding average (**FA**) after two games is:

*(See page 37 for how to compute your **FA**)*

When I was on deck, waiting for my first turn at bat, I felt: _____

_____

_____

For me, the most challenging thing about batting is:_____

_____

MY TEAM'S RECORD IS NOW

WINS   LOSSES

_____ VS. _____

_____ _____

WINNING AND LOSING PITCHERS

_____Won

_____Lost

IF YOU PITCHED, HOW WELL DID YOU DO?

I pitched _____ innings.

I struck out _____ batters,

walked _____ batters,

gave up _____ hits,

and _____ earned runs.

My earned run average (**ERA**) after two games is:

*(See page 35 for how to compute your **ERA**)*

TEAMS · SCORE

_____ (HOME) VS.

STARTING PITCHERS · THROWS R/L

_____ VS. _____

WINNING AND LOSING PITCHERS

_____ Won

_____ Lost

IF YOU PITCHED, HOW WELL DID YOU DO?

I pitched _____ innings.

I struck out _____ batters,

walked _____ batters,

gave up _____ hits,

and _____ earned runs.

My earned run average (**ERA**) after three games is:

(See page 35 for how to compute your **ERA**)

The most exciting part of the game came in the _____

_____ inning. Here's what happened:

_____

_____

_____

MY TEAM'S RECORD IS NOW

WINS   LOSSES

When I'm playing my position in the field, I feel:

_____

_____

_____

_____

Q. Which will travel faster, a ground ball hit in Minnesota's Metrodome or one hit in L.A.'s Dodger Stadium?

A. A grounder hit in Minnesota's Metrodome will travel faster because the infield there is covered with artificial turf which offers less resistance to a rolling ball.

IN THE FIELD

I played *(name position[s])* _____ .

    I had _____ fielding chances.

    I made _____ fielding errors.

    I made _____ throwing errors.

My fielding average (FA) after three games is:

(See page 37 for how to compute your FA)

CHART YOUR HITS (See page 47 for how to chart your hits.)

HOT TIP! **FIELDING**

Catch any ball above your waist with the fingers of your glove pointing up or to the side.

Catch any ball below your waist with the fingers of your glove pointing down. Use two hands.

MY AT BATS

I batted _____ times.

I got _____ hits,

I walked _____ times, and

batted in _____ teammates.

I struck out _____ times,

grounded out _____ times, and

popped out _____ times.

My batting average (AVG) after three games is:

(See page 39 for how to compute your AVG)

TEAMS   SCORE

_____ (HOME) VS.

_____

STARTING PITCHERS   THROWS R/L

_____ VS. _____

The most exciting part of the game came in the

_____ inning. Here's what happened:

_____

_____

_____

_____

When I'm on the bench, these are some of the

things I do: _____

_____

WINNING AND LOSING PITCHERS

_____ Won

_____ Lost

IF YOU PITCHED, HOW WELL DID YOU DO?

_____

I pitched _____ innings.

I struck out _____ batters,

walked _____ batters,

gave up _____ hits,

and _____ earned runs.

My earned run average (ERA) after four games is:

(See page 35 for how to compute your ERA)

HOT TIP!

BASE COACHING

**When coaching third base, know
when to use these signals:**

STOP   SLIDE   KEEP
                             GOING

MY TEAM'S RECORD IS NOW

WINS   LOSSES

MY AT BATS

I batted _____ times.

I got _____ hits,

I walked _____ times, and

batted in _____ teammates.

I struck out _____ times,

grounded out _____ times, and

popped out _____ times.

My batting average (**AVG**) after four games is:

*(See page 39 for how to compute your **AVG**)*

IN THE FIELD

I played *(name position[s])* _____ .

I had _____ fielding chances.

I made _____ fielding errors.

I made _____ throwing errors.

My fielding average (**FA**) after four games is:

*(See page 37 for how to compute your **FA**)*

After today's game I *(describe what you did after the game)*:

_____

_____

_____

_____

_____

DID YOU KNOW...

The first major-league player to steal more than 100 bases in a single season was Maury Wills of the Los Angeles Dodgers. Wills stole 104 bases in 1962.

TEAMS　　　　　　　　SCORE

_____ (HOME) VS.

_____

STARTING PITCHERS　　THROWS R/L

_____ VS. _____

_____ _____

WINNING AND LOSING PITCHERS

_____Won

_____Lost

The most exciting part of the game came in the

_____ inning. Here's what happened:

_____

_____

_____

_____

_____

MY TEAM'S RECORD IS NOW

WINS　LOSSES

This is how I would describe our team after five games. In the field:_____

_____

_____

At bat:_____

_____

_____

_____

IF YOU PITCHED, HOW WELL DID YOU DO?

I pitched _____ innings.

I struck out _____ batters,

walked _____ batters,

gave up _____ hits,

and _____ earned runs.

My earned run average (**ERA**) after five games is:

(See page 35 for how to compute your **ERA**)

CHART YOUR HITS (See page 47 for how to chart your hits.)

Q. What is a "seeing-eye single"?

A. A ground ball that just threads its way between infielders for a hit.

IN THE FIELD

I played *(name position[s])* _____.

I had _____ fielding chances.

I made _____ fielding errors.

I made _____ throwing errors.

My fielding average **(FA)** after five games is:

(See page 37 for how to compute your FA)

MY AT BATS

I batted _____ times.

I got _____ hits,

I walked _____ times, and

batted in _____ teammates.

I struck out _____ times,

grounded out _____ times, and

popped out _____ times.

My batting average **(AVG)** after five games is:

(See page 39 for how to compute your AVG)

6

TEAMS	SCORE
_____ (HOME) VS.	
_____	

MY TEAM'S RECORD IS NOW

WINS   LOSSES

CHART YOUR HITS (See page 47 for how to chart your hits.)

The most exciting part of the game came in the

_____ inning. Here's what happened:

_____

_____

_____

MY AT BATS

I batted _____ times.

I got _____ hits,

I walked _____ times, and

batted in _____ teammates.

I struck out _____ times,

grounded out _____ times, and

popped out _____ times.

My batting average (AVG) after six games is:

(See page 39 for how to compute your **AVG**)

IN THE FIELD

I played *(name position[s])* _____ .

    I had _____ fielding chances.

    I made _____ fielding errors.

    I made _____ throwing errors.

    My fielding average **(FA)** after six games is:

*(See page 37 for how to compute your **FA**)*

If I were teaching new players how to bat, this

is what I would tell them: _____

_____

_____

HOT TIP!

BATTING

When batting, position your feet so that when you extend the bat, it covers the entire width of the strike zone.

_____

_____

_____

_____

STARTING PITCHERS   **THROWS R/L**

_____ vs. _____

_____ _____

WINNING AND LOSING PITCHERS

_____Won

_____Lost

IF YOU PITCHED, HOW WELL DID YOU DO?

    I pitched _____ innings.

I struck out _____ batters,

    walked _____ batters,

    gave up _____ hits,

    and _____ earned runs.

  My earned run average **(ERA)** after six games is:

*(See page 35 for how to compute your **ERA**)*

21

TEAMS **SCORE**

_____ (HOME) VS.

_____

STARTING PITCHERS **THROWS R/L**

_____ VS. _____

_____ _____

WINNING AND LOSING PITCHERS

_____ Won

_____ Lost

If I were a sportswriter, I would use these words to describe these baseball sensations:

The smell of my glove_____

_____

The sound of the ball when it hits my glove

_____

The feeling I get when I connect with a good hit

_____

The sound of the crowd when my team scores

_____

_____

IF YOU PITCHED, HOW WELL DID YOU DO?

I pitched _____ innings.

I struck out _____ batters,

walked _____ batters,

gave up _____ hits,

and _____ earned runs.

My earned run average (**ERA**) after seven games is:

(See page 35 for how to compute your **ERA**)

MY TEAM'S RECORD IS NOW

WINS   LOSSES

MY AT BATS

I batted _____ times.

I got _____ hits,

I walked _____ times, and

batted in _____ teammates.

I struck out _____ times,

grounded out _____ times, and

popped out _____ times.

My batting average (**AVG**) after seven games is:

(See page 39 for how to compute your **AVG***)*

IN THE FIELD

I played *(name position[s])* _____ .

I had _____ fielding chances.

I made _____ fielding errors.

I made _____ throwing errors.

My fielding average (**FA**) after seven games is:

(See page 37 for how to compute your **FA***)*

The most exciting part of the game came in the

_____ inning. Here's what happened:

_____

_____

_____

_____

23

TEAMS

SCORE

_____ (HOME) VS.

_____

HOT TIP!

CATCHING

If you're a catcher, squat. Don't kneel. When waiting for a pitch, give your pitcher a good target with your glove and keep your bare hand either behind the glove or in a fist behind your back.

CHART YOUR HITS (See page 47 for how to chart your hits.)

The most exciting part of the game came in the _____ inning. Here's what happened:

_____

_____

_____

_____

_____

MY AT BATS

I batted _____ times.

I got _____ hits,

I walked _____ times, and

batted in _____ teammates.

I struck out _____ times,

grounded out _____ times, and

popped out _____ times.

My batting average (**AVG**) after eight games is:

(See page 39 for how to compute your **AVG**)

IN THE FIELD

I played *(name position[s])* _____ .

    I had _____ fielding chances.

    I made _____ fielding errors.

    I made _____ throwing errors.

My fielding average **(FA)** after eight games is:

*(See page 37 for how to compute your **FA**)*

I am a better player than I was at the start of the season. Here's how and why: _____

_____

_____

Here's where I can still improve: _____

_____

_____

MY TEAM'S RECORD IS NOW

WINS   LOSSES

_____ VS. _____

_____   _____

WINNING AND LOSING PITCHERS

_____ Won

_____ Lost

IF YOU PITCHED, HOW WELL DID YOU DO?

    I pitched _____ innings.

I struck out _____ batters,

    walked _____ batters,

    gave up _____ hits,

    and _____ earned runs.

My earned run average **(ERA)** after eight games is:

*(See page 35 for how to compute your **ERA**)*

TEAMS | SCORE

_____ (HOME) VS.

_____

STARTING PITCHERS | THROWS R/L

_____ VS. _____

_____ _____

WINNING AND LOSING PITCHERS

_____ Won

_____ Lost

The most exciting part of the game came in the

_____ inning. Here's what happened:

_____

_____

_____

_____

_____

MY TEAM'S RECORD IS NOW

WINS   LOSSES

Every batter occasionally has an off day or a

slump. My low point was: _____

_____

_____

To get out of my slump, I: _____

_____

_____

_____

IF YOU PITCHED, HOW WELL DID YOU DO?

I pitched _____ innings.

I struck out _____ batters,

walked _____ batters,

gave up _____ hits,

and _____ earned runs.

My earned run average (**ERA**) after nine games is:

(See page 35 for how to compute your **ERA**)

CHART YOUR HITS (See page 47 for how to chart your hits.)

Q. What is a "Texas-Leaguer"?

A. A pop fly that drops behind the infield for a hit, usually a single (also known as a banjo, bleeder, blooper, looper, plunker, pooper, or squibbler). The term originated in 1889 to describe a type of hit common in the old Texas League.

MY AT BATS

I batted _____ times.

I got _____ hits,

I walked _____ times, and

batted in _____ teammates.

I struck out _____ times,

grounded out _____ times, and

popped out _____ times.

My batting average **(AVG)** after nine games is:

(See page 39 for how to compute your **AVG**)

IN THE FIELD

I played _(name position[s])_ _____ .

I had _____ fielding chances.

I made _____ fielding errors.

I made _____ throwing errors.

My fielding average **(FA)** after nine games is:

(See page 37 for how to compute your **FA**)

TEAMS · SCORE

_____ (HOME) VS. [ ]

_____ [ ]

STARTING PITCHERS · THROWS R/L

_____ VS. _____

_____ _____

The most exciting part of the game came in the

_____ inning. Here's what happened:

_____

_____

_____

_____

A major-league scouting report would say

this about me as a baseball player.

As a fielder:_____

_____

_____

As a batter:_____

_____

_____

WINNING AND LOSING PITCHERS

_____Won

_____Lost

IF YOU PITCHED, HOW WELL DID YOU DO?

I pitched _____ innings.

I struck out _____ batters,

walked _____ batters,

gave up _____ hits,

and _____ earned runs.

My earned run average (**ERA**) after ten games is:

[ ]

*(See page 35 for how to compute your **ERA**)*

MY TEAM'S RECORD IS NOW

[ ] [ ]

WINS LOSSES

CHART YOUR HITS (See page 47 for how to chart your hits.)

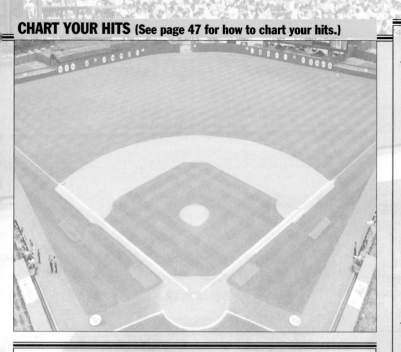

MY AT BATS

I batted _____ times.

I got _____ hits,

I walked _____ times, and

batted in _____ teammates.

I struck out _____ times,

grounded out _____ times, and

popped out _____ times.

My batting average **(AVG)** after ten games is:

*(See page 39 for how to compute your **AVG**)*

IN THE FIELD

I played *(name position[s])* _____.

I had _____ fielding chances.

I made _____ fielding errors.

I made _____ throwing errors.

My fielding average **(FA)** after ten games is:

*(See page 37 for how to compute your **FA**)*

OUTFIELD

When fielding a ground ball as an outfielder, drop to one knee and block the ball with your glove, hand, leg, foot, and chest. Remember: an outfielder is the last line of defense. Try to never let a ground ball get past you.

TEAMS	SCORE
(HOME) VS.	

MY TEAM'S RECORD IS NOW

WINS   LOSSES

CHART YOUR HITS (See page 47 for how to chart your hits.)

The most exciting part of the game came in the _____ inning. Here's what happened:

_____

_____

_____

_____

MY AT BATS

I batted _____ times.

I got _____ hits,

I walked _____ times, and

batted in _____ teammates.

I struck out _____ times,

grounded out _____ times, and

popped out _____ times.

My batting average (**AVG**) after eleven games is:

*(See page 39 for how to compute your **AVG**)*

IN THE FIELD

I played *(name position[s])* _____ .

I had _____ fielding chances.

I made _____ fielding errors.

I made _____ throwing errors.

My fielding average (**FA**) after eleven games is:

[ ]

*(See page 37 for how to compute your **FA**)*

My idea of a great way to celebrate when our team wins is: _____

_____

_____

WINNING AND LOSING PITCHERS	

_____ Won

_____ Lost

IF YOU PITCHED, HOW WELL DID YOU DO?

I pitched _____ innings.

I struck out _____ batters,

walked _____ batters,

gave up _____ hits,

and _____ earned runs.

My earned run average (**ERA**) after eleven games is:

[ ]

*(See page 35 for how to compute your **ERA**)*

TEAMS · SCORE

_____ (HOME) VS.

_____

STARTING PITCHERS · THROWS R/L

_____ VS. _____

_____ _____

WINNING AND LOSING PITCHERS

_____ Won

_____ Lost

The most exciting part of the game came in the

_____ inning. Here's what happened:

_____

_____

_____

_____

_____

_____

IF YOU PITCHED, HOW WELL DID YOU DO?

I pitched _____ innings.

I struck out _____ batters,

walked _____ batters,

gave up _____ hits,

and _____ earned runs.

My earned run average (**ERA**) after twelve games is:

(See page 35 for how to compute your **ERA**)

MY TEAM'S RECORD IS NOW

WINS   LOSSES

IN THE FIELD

I played *(name position[s])* _____ .

I had _____ fielding chances.

I made _____ fielding errors.

I made _____ throwing errors.

My fielding average (**FA**) after twelve games is:

[ ]

*(See page 37 for how to compute your **FA**)*

CHART YOUR HITS (See page 47 for how to chart your hits.)

Q. What is a "wheel-house" and a "can of corn"?

A. A wheelhouse is the place in the strike zone where a batter makes best contact with a ball. Every batter has his own wheel-house. A can of corn is a pitch that comes into a batter's wheelhouse and is easy to hit. Also known as a fat pitch or a gopher ball.

MY AT BATS

I batted _____ times.

I got _____ hits,

I walked _____ times, and

batted in _____ teammates.

I struck out _____ times,

grounded out _____ times, and

popped out _____ times.

My batting average (**AVG**) after twelve games is:

[ ]

*(See page 39 for how to compute your **AVG**)*

My Stats by Game

Batting

	NAME OF OPPOSING TEAM	AVERAGE (AVG)	AT BATS (AB)	RUNS I SCORED (R)	SINGLES (1B)	DOUBLES (2B)	TRIPLES (3B)	HOME RUNS (HR)	BASES ON BALLS (BB)	STRIKEOUTS (SO)	RUNS BATTED IN (RBI)
1	vs										
2	vs										
3	vs										
4	vs										
5	vs										
6	vs										
7	vs										
8	vs										
9	vs										
10	vs										
11	vs										
12	vs										
	My Season Totals ▶										

HOW TO COMPUTE YOUR EARNED RUN AVERAGE

1. Start by multiplying the total number of earned runs (**ER**) you have given up by the number 6, which is the number of innings (**I**) in an average Little League game.
2. Divide that total by the actual number of innings you have pitched (**IP**). The result is your earned run average (**ERA**). It can be shown by this equation: $ER \times 6(I) \div IP = ERA$

For example, say you have given up 10 earned runs and have pitched a total of 20 innings. To compute your ERA, you would multiply 10 (**ER**) by 6 (**I**), and divide the result, which is 60, by 20 (**IP**).

$$\begin{array}{r} 3.00 = \textbf{ERA} \\ \text{(innings pitched } \textbf{IP}\text{) } 20\overline{\smash)60.00} \text{ (earned runs } \textbf{ER}\text{)} \\ \underline{-60} \\ 0 \end{array}$$

Your Earned Run Average Is
3.00

That means, on average as a pitcher, you give up 3 runs a game.

Fielding

AVERAGE (AVG)	GAMES PLAYED (G)	PUT-OUTS (PO)	ASSISTS (A)	FIELDING ERRORS (FE)	THROWING ERRORS (TE)

Pitching

INNINGS PITCHED (IP)	STRIKEOUTS (SO)	WALKS (BB)	HITS (H)	RUNS (R)	EARNED RUNS (ER)	EARNED RUN AVERAGE (ERA)

My Fielding Totals

This is how well I fielded this season.

GAMES PLAYED G	PUT-OUTS PO	ASSISTS A	FIELDING ERRORS FE	THROWING ERRORS TE

If your season's fielding average is:

ABOVE   .800 YOU'RE A GOLD GLOVE FIELDER

BETWEEN .600 AND .800 YOU'RE AN ALL-STAR FIELDER

BETWEEN .400 AND .600 YOU'RE A JOURNEYMAN FIELDER

BELOW   .400 YOU'RE A UTILITY FIELDER

MY FIELDING AVERAGE IS

My best fielding play of the season was: _____

_____

_____

_____

_____

After making the play I felt: _____

_____

_____

HOW TO COMPUTE YOUR FIELDING AVERAGE

A put-out (**PO**) is when you catch a fly ball, or tag a base on a force, or tag a runner. An assist (**A**) is when you catch or field a ball during a play that leads to an out. A fielding average (**FA**) is a player's total number of put-outs plus assists divided by the player's total number of put-outs plus assists plus errors.

1. Start by adding your total number of put-outs (**PO**) plus assists (**A**).
2. Divide that number by your total number of put-outs (**PO**) plus assists (**A**) plus errors (**E**). The result of dividing the first number by the second number is your fielding average (**FA**). It can be expressed by this equation:

$$(\text{PO} + \text{A}) \div (\text{PO} + \text{A} + \text{E}) = \text{FA}$$

For example, say you have 2 put-outs, 6 assists, and 2 errors. Add 2 (**PO**) and 6 (**A**) together and divide that number (8) by the number you get when you add 2 (**PO**), 6 (**A**), and 2 (**E**), which is 10.

$$\begin{array}{r} .800 = \textbf{FA} \\ (\textbf{PO} + \textbf{A} + \textbf{E})\ 10\overline{\smash{\big)}\ 8.000}\ (\textbf{PO} + \textbf{A}) \\ \underline{-8\ 0} \\ 0 \end{array}$$

Your Fielding Average Is
.800

My Batting Totals

My best hit of the season was:_____

_____

_____

_____

_____

After I got the hit I felt:_____

_____

_____

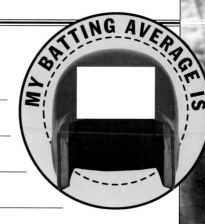

MY BATTING AVERAGE IS

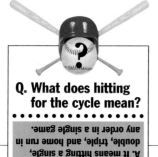

Q. What does hitting for the cycle mean?
• • • • • • • • • • • • •

A. It means hitting a single, double, triple, and home run in any order in a single game.

HOW TO COMPUTE YOUR SLUGGING AVERAGE

1. Start by adding your total number of bases (**TB**) that you reached by your own hits. Do not include bases reached on walks (**BB**) or errors (**E**).
2. Divide that number by your total number of at bats (**AB**). Here, too, do not include the times you walked (**BB**) or reached a base on an error. Those do not count as at bats.
3. The result of dividing total bases (**TB**) by at bats (**AB**) is your slugging average (**SA**). It can be expressed by this equation:

$$TB \div AB = SA$$

For example, let's say you had 10 at bats and got two hits: a single and a triple. Your total bases number is 4 (1 base for the single, 3 for the triple. 1+3=4 total bases). To compute your slugging average, you would divide your 10 at bats into those 4 total bases, like this:

```
              .400 = SA
          _____
(at bats AB) 10 | 4.000 (total bases TB)
             −4 0
          _____
                0
```

Your Slugging Average Is
.400

MY SLUGGING AVERAGE IS

This is how well I batted this season.

AT BATS **AB**	RUNS I SCORED **R**	SINGLES **1B**	DOUBLES **2B**	TRIPLES **3B**	HOME RUNS **HR**	BASES ON BALLS **BB**	STRIKEOUTS **SO**	RUNS I BATTED IN **RBI**

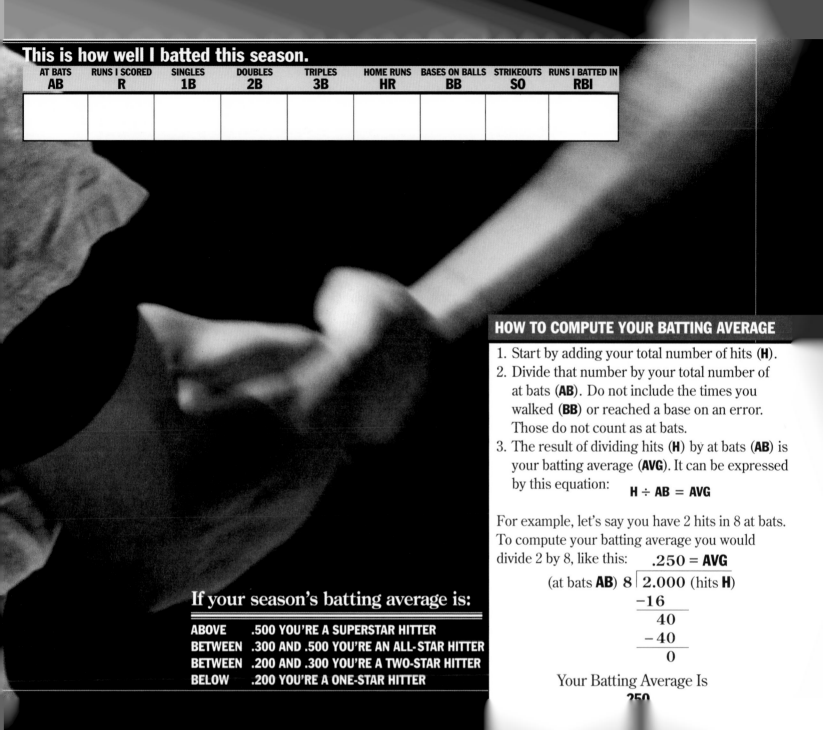

HOW TO COMPUTE YOUR BATTING AVERAGE

1. Start by adding your total number of hits (**H**).
2. Divide that number by your total number of at bats (**AB**). Do not include the times you walked (**BB**) or reached a base on an error. Those do not count as at bats.
3. The result of dividing hits (**H**) by at bats (**AB**) is your batting average (**AVG**). It can be expressed by this equation: $H \div AB = AVG$

For example, let's say you have 2 hits in 8 at bats. To compute your batting average you would divide 2 by 8, like this:

$$
\begin{array}{r}
.250 = \textbf{AVG} \\
\text{(at bats } \textbf{AB}) \; 8 \; \overline{\smash{\big)}\; 2.000 \; \text{(hits } \textbf{H})} \\
\underline{-16} \\
40 \\
\underline{-40} \\
0
\end{array}
$$

Your Batting Average Is
250

If your season's batting average is:

ABOVE	.500 YOU'RE A SUPERSTAR HITTER
BETWEEN	.300 AND .500 YOU'RE AN ALL-STAR HITTER
BETWEEN	.200 AND .300 YOU'RE A TWO-STAR HITTER
BELOW	.200 YOU'RE A ONE-STAR HITTER

How I Compare to the All-Time Best

Compare your season's batting, slugging, and pitching averages to those of the all-time single-season leaders in the major leagues. How do you rate?

Batting Average

NAME	TEAM	LEAGUE	YEAR	AVERAGE
1. Rogers Hornsby	St. L.	NL	1924	.424
2. Nap Lajoie	Phi.	AL	1901	.422
3. Ty Cobb	Det.	AL	1911	.420
(tie) George Sisler	St. L.	AL	1922	.420
5. Ty Cobb	Det.	AL	1912	.410
6. Joe Jackson	Cle.	AL	1911	.408
7. George Sisler	St. L.	AL	1920	.407
8. Ted Williams	Bos.	AL	1941	.406
9. Rogers Hornsby	St. L.	NL	1925	.403
(tie) Harry Heilmann	Det.	AL	1923	.403

Slugging Average

NAME	TEAM	LEAGUE	YEAR	AVERAGE
1. Babe Ruth	NY	AL	1920	.847
2. Babe Ruth	NY	AL	1921	.846
3. Babe Ruth	NY	AL	1927	.777
4. Lou Gehrig	NY	AL	1927	.765
5. Babe Ruth	NY	AL	1923	.764
6. Rogers Hornsby	St. L.	NL	1925	.756
7. Jimmie Foxx	Phi.	AL	1932	.749
8. Babe Ruth	NY	AL	1924	.739
9. Babe Ruth	NY	AL	1926	.737
10. Ted Williams	Bos.	AL	1941	.735

Earned Run Average

NAME	TEAM	LEAGUE	YEAR	AVERAGE
1. Dutch Leonard	Bos.	AL	1914	1.01
2. Mordecai Brown	Chi.	NL	1906	1.04
3. Bob Gibson	St. L.	NL	1968	1.12
4. Christy Mathewson	NY	NL	1909	1.14
(tie) Walter Johnson	Was.	AL	1913	1.14
6. Jack Pfeister	Chi.	NL	1907	1.15
7. Addie Joss	Cle.	AL	1908	1.16
8. Carl Lundgren	Chi.	NL	1907	1.17
9. Grover Alexander	Phi.	NL	1915	1.22
10. Cy Young	Bos.	AL	1908	1.26

DID YOU KNOW...

Ted Williams, Hall-of-Fame leftfielder for the Boston Red Sox, was the last major leaguer to bat over .400 in a single season. In 1941, Williams, also known as The Kid, The Splendid Splinter, and Teddy Ballgame, hit .406.

Q. What is a perfect game?

A A no-hit, no-run game in which no opposing baserunner reaches first base.

My Personal Collection of Baseball Tips and Tricks

All baseball players have their own assortment of tips and tricks to help them play the game better. These are mine for:

Batting:_____

Fielding:_____

Baserunning:_____

Throwing:_____

Pitching:_____

Sliding:_____

Others:_____

_____

_____

The best advice I ever received as a player was from:

_____

who said: _____

_____

_____

Me and My Dream Team

If I could play baseball with any major-league players past or present, this is what my starting lineup would look like *(be sure to include yourself in the lineup)***:**

PLAYER'S NAME (BATTING ORDER)	POSITION	WHY I CHOSE THIS PLAYER
1.		
2.		
3.		
4.		
5.		
6.		
7.		
8.		
9.		

My Dream Ballpark

If I could build my dream ballpark, it would look like this *(Draw a picture of your dream ballpark, showing its overall shape and seating plan. Be sure to show any special features, such as dugouts, clubhouses, bullpens, soda machines, and so on. You can use the symbols shown below.)*:

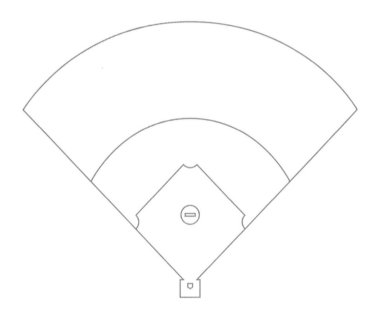

DID YOU KNOW...

The average number of baseballs used in a major-league game is 60. Supplied by the home team, the balls are rubbed with a special mud called Lena Blackburne's Baseball Rubbing Mud which makes the balls more visible and less slippery. Cost of the mud: $75 a can!

Memorable Baseball Days

Use this section to write about baseball days that were especially memorable to you. Maybe you had a fun catch with a parent, or an exciting day at a major league game. Or maybe you visited the Baseball Hall of Fame and Museum in Cooperstown, New York, or went to a team party. Whatever the day was, tell why it was memorable to you, using your own thoughts and words.

WHEN AND WHERE:

WHEN AND WHERE:

WHEN AND WHERE:

Describe your own best game of the season, and why.

DATE: _____

AGAINST: _____

_____

_____

_____

_____

_____

_____

_____

WHEN AND WHERE: _____

✍ _____

_____

_____

_____

WHEN AND WHERE: _____

✍ _____

_____

_____

_____

Clippings and Stuff from
My Baseball Season

Paste on these pages any photos, newspaper
clippings, ticket stubs, or other items to help
remember your season by.

How to Chart Your Hits
Charting your hits is simple if you use these symbols:

Short, squiggly line   ∿∿∿   = BUNT

Long, squiggly line   ∿∿∿∿∿   = GROUND BALL

Smooth, curved line   ⌢   = FLY BALL

Draw a box at the end of each line to tell what kind of hit you got:

1B	= Single	3B	= Triple
2B	= Double	HR	= Home Run

- -

You can also use a box to show how an out was made against you. For example:

4 – 3 = A ball hit to 4, the second baseman, who threw to 3, the first baseman, for the out.

F – 7 = A fly ball (F) caught by 7, the left fielder, for the out.

E – 6 = Error (E) by 6, the shortstop, allowed you to reach base.

- -

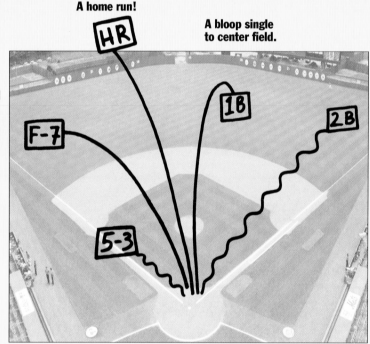

A home run!

A bloop single to center field.

Fly ball to left field, caught for an out.

A ground ball double to right.

A bunt fielded by the third baseman (5) and thrown to the first baseman (3) for an out.

My Three Favorite Players

1._____

2._____

3._____

I like_____ best

because _____

_____

Of all the things that happened this baseball

season, what I'll always remember is:_____

_____

_____

_____

_____

_____

CREDITS

WRITING AND PHOTOGRAPHY: **Tom Ettinger, Bill Jaspersohn**
DESIGN: **Joseph Lee (HOPKINS/BAUMANN)**
ILLUSTRATIONS: **ACME DESIGN COMPANY**
PICTURE CREDITS: player portrait, p.2: courtesy Matthew Hommeyer; team photo, p.3: Mike Coburn; p.18, 26, 36, 39, 41: Walter Iooss, Jr.; Ted Williams, p.40: the National Baseball Hall of Fame and Museum. All other photos by Tom Ettinger and Bill Jaspersohn.
SPECIAL THANKS TO: **the Baltimore Orioles, the Boston Red Sox, the New York Mets, the St. Louis Cardinals, the Trumbull (Connecticut) Nationals.**

DID YOU KNOW...

Lou Gehrig, first baseman for the New York Yankees from 1923 to 1939, played in a record 2,130 consecutive games and was dubbed the "Iron Horse."

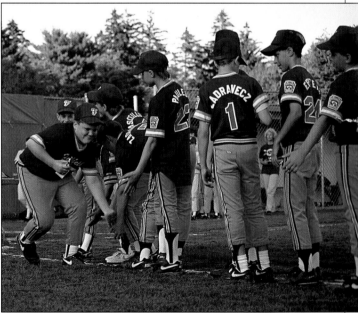